COOL CARS

LAMBORGHINI
SIAN

BY THOMAS K. ADAMSON

EPIC

BELLWETHER MEDIA ››› MINNEAPOLIS, MN

EPIC BOOKS are no ordinary books. They burst with intense action, high-speed heroics, and shadows of the unknown. Are you ready for an Epic adventure?

This edition first published in 2023 by Bellwether Media, Inc.

No part of this publication may be reproduced in whole or in part without written permission of the publisher. For information regarding permission, write to Bellwether Media, Inc., Attention: Permissions Department, 6012 Blue Circle Drive, Minnetonka, MN 55343.

Library of Congress Cataloging-in-Publication Data

LC record for Lamborghini Sián available at: https://lccn.loc.gov/2022020218

Text copyright © 2023 by Bellwether Media, Inc. EPIC and associated logos are trademarks and/or registered trademarks of Bellwether Media, Inc.

Editor: Kieran Downs   Designer: Jeffrey Kollock

Printed in the United States of America, North Mankato, MN

TABLE OF CONTENTS

LIGHTNING IN A SPORTS CAR	4
ALL ABOUT THE SIÁN	6
PARTS OF THE SIÁN	12
THE SIÁN'S FUTURE	20
GLOSSARY	22
TO LEARN MORE	23
INDEX	24

LIGHTNING IN A SPORTS CAR »

A Lamborghini Sián rolls onto the road. It looks like it came from the future.

The driver revs the engine. It makes a loud growl. The Sián is one flashy car!

LIGHTNING FAST

Sián means "flash of lighting" in Bolognese.

ALL ABOUT THE SIÁN »

LAMBORGHINI FACTORY IN SANT'AGATA BOLOGNESE, ITALY

Lamborghini began in 1963. Its cars are made in Sant'Agata Bolognese, Italy.

Famous Lamborghini **models** include the Countach and the Aventador SVJ. The Sián uses many of the same design ideas as these cars.

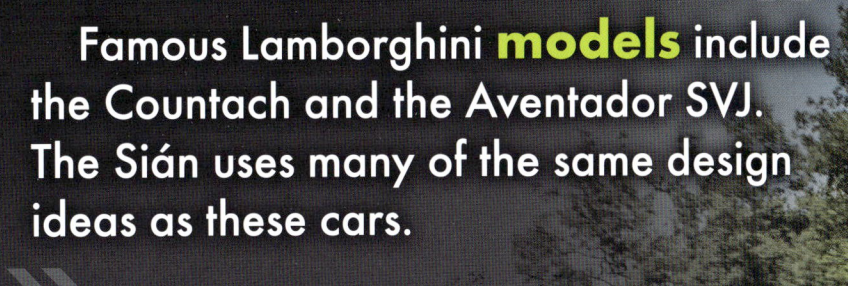

COUNTACH

📍 WHERE IS IT MADE?

EUROPE

SANT'AGATA BOLOGNESE, ITALY

The Sián is Lamborghini's first **hybrid** car. It has a gas engine with an **electric** boost.

Its engine produces 808 **horsepower**. It is the most powerful engine in a Lamborghini road car.

Lamborghini did not make many Siáns. Only 63 **coupe** models were made. They also made 19 **roadster** models. The cars sold out the minute they went on sale.

LAMBORGHINI HISTORY

The 19 roadsters and 63 coupes stand for the year 1963. That is the year Lamborghini started.

SIÁN ROADSTER

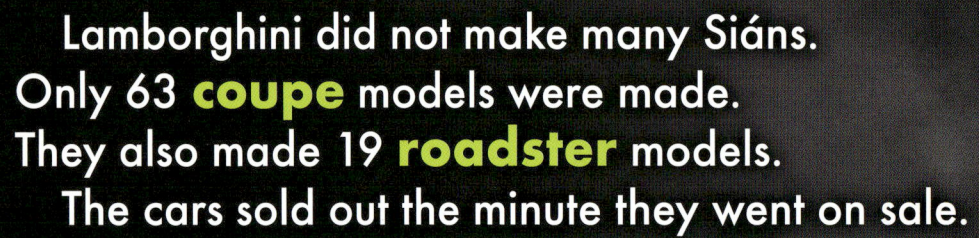

SIÁN BASICS

YEAR FIRST MADE — 2019

COST — starts around $3 million

HOW MANY MADE — 63 coupes; 19 roadsters

FEATURES

V12 engine

supercapacitor

vent flaps

PARTS OF THE SIÁN »

The Sián has Y-shaped headlights. Triple taillights line the back of the car. The body is made of **carbon fiber**. The doors open upward. They are known as scissor doors.

ENGINE SPECS

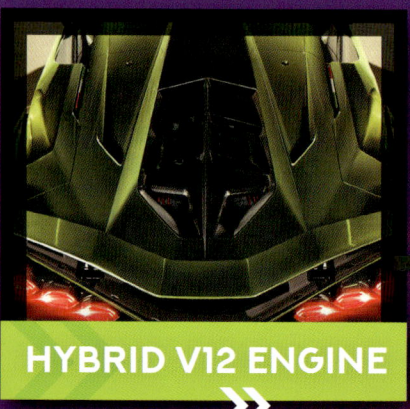

HYBRID V12 ENGINE »

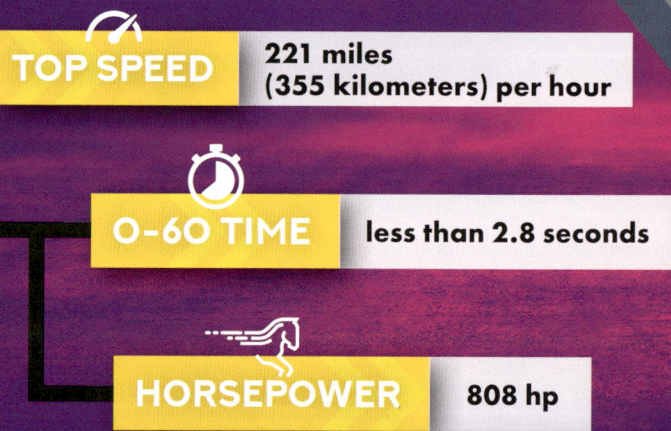

TOP SPEED	221 miles (355 kilometers) per hour
0-60 TIME	less than 2.8 seconds
HORSEPOWER	808 hp

Most hybrid cars use heavy **batteries**. The Sián has a **supercapacitor** instead. This part stores **energy**.

It releases energy quickly when the gas pedal is pressed. Stepping on the brakes recharges it.

The Sian's big **V12 engine** gives it most of its power. The electric **motor** gives it extra power. The car reaches 60 miles (97 kilometers) per hour in less than 2.8 seconds!

V12 ENGINE

The engine shifts gears smoothly. But it still growls!

The Sián has vent flaps on the back. They open when the engine heats up. This helps cool the engine.

VENT FLAPS
Lamborghini
Sián

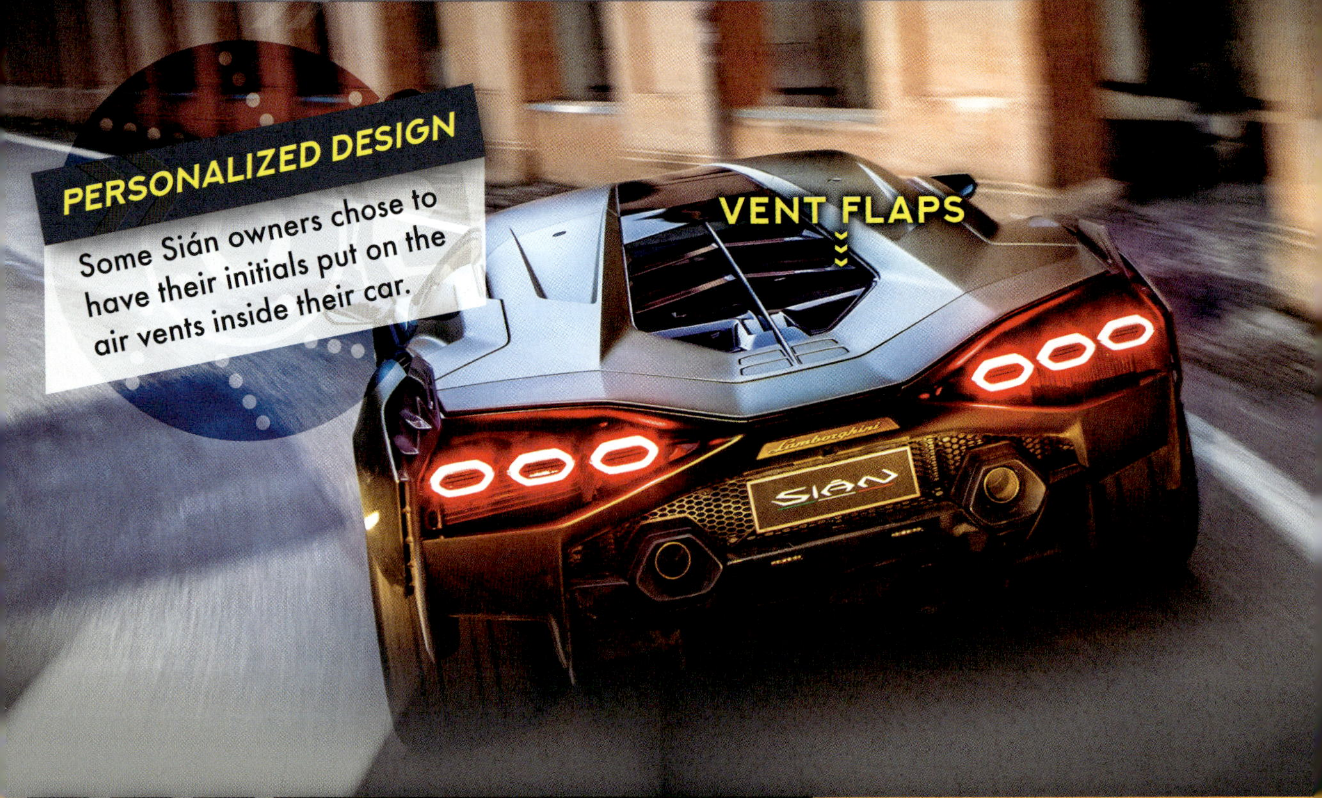

PERSONALIZED DESIGN

Some Sián owners chose to have their initials put on the air vents inside their car.

SIZE CHART

WIDTH
81.9 inches
(208 centimeters)
Sián

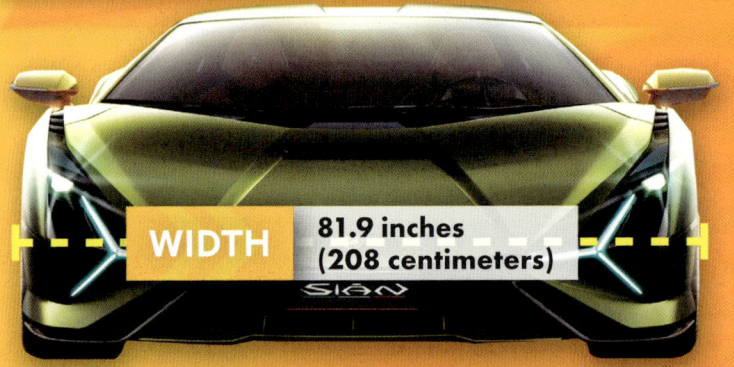

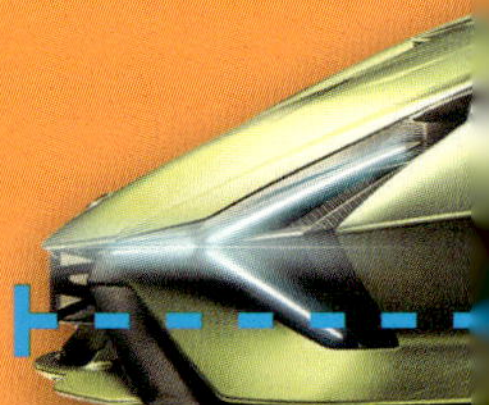

The flaps are **sensitive** to heat. They open on their own!

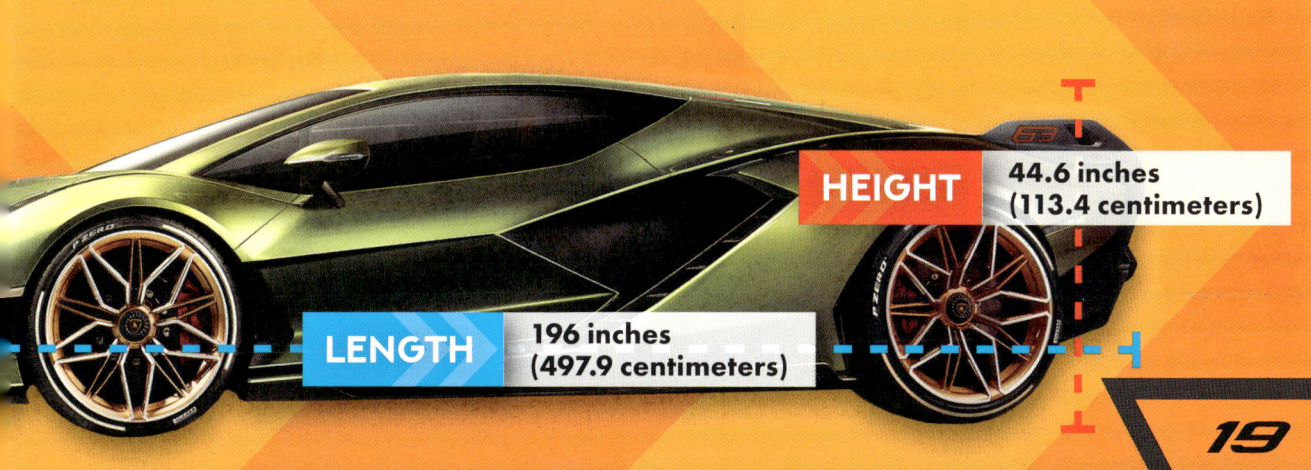

LENGTH 196 inches (497.9 centimeters)

HEIGHT 44.6 inches (113.4 centimeters)

THE SIÁN'S FUTURE »

Lamborghini does not plan on making more Siáns. But they will make more hybrid cars in the future.

The Sián was Lamborghini's first hybrid car. But it will not be its last!

LEGO LAMBO

LEGO created a life-size model of the Sián coupe. It uses more than 400,000 pieces. Its headlights and taillights both light up!

LEGO TECHNIC SIÁN

GLOSSARY

batteries—parts that supply energy to electric cars

carbon fiber—a strong, lightweight material used to strengthen things

coupe—a car with a hard roof and two doors

electric—able to run without gasoline

energy—usable power that comes from things including heat, electricity, and sound

horsepower—a measurement of the power of an engine or motor

hybrid—using both a gasoline engine and an electric motor for power

models—specific types of cars

motor—a machine that causes something to move

roadster—a two-seated car with an open top

sensitive—able to quickly react to changes

supercapacitor—a device that stores and releases energy rapidly

V12 engine—an engine with 12 cylinders arranged in the shape of a "V"

TO LEARN MORE

AT THE LIBRARY

Adamson, Thomas K. *Lamborghini Huracán Evo*. Minneapolis, Minn.: Bellwether Media, 2023.

Geddis, Norm. *Hop Inside the Most Exotic Cars*. Broomall, Pa.: Mason Crest, 2019.

Storm, Marysa. *Supercars*. Mankato, Minn.: Black Rabbit Books, 2020.

ON THE WEB

Factsurfer.com gives you a safe, fun way to find more information.

1. Go to www.factsurfer.com.

2. Enter "Lamborghini Sián" into the search box and click 🔍.

3. Select your book cover to see a list of related content.

INDEX

basics, 11
batteries, 14
body, 12
brakes, 15
carbon fiber, 12, 13
company, 6, 7, 8, 9, 10, 20
coupe, 10, 20
design, 7
doors, 12
electric, 8, 16
energy, 14, 15
engine, 5, 8, 9, 12, 16, 17, 18
engine specs, 12
headlights, 12, 13, 20
history, 6, 10
horsepower, 9
hybrid, 8, 14, 20
LEGO, 20
models, 7, 10, 20

motor, 16
name, 5
number, 10
roadster, 10
sales, 10
Sant'Agata Bolognese, Italy, 6, 7
size chart, 18–19
speed, 16
supercapacitor, 14, 15
taillights, 12, 20
vent flaps, 18, 19

The images in this book are reproduced through the courtesy of: Lamborghini, front cover, pp. 1, 3, 4, 4-5, 6, 6-7, 8-9, 9, 10-11, 11-12 (engine), 11 (supercapacitor, vent), 12-13, 14-15 (left), 14-15 (right), 16-17 (left), 16-17 (right), 18-19 (left), 18 (width), 18-19 (length), 19, 20-21 (left), 20-21 (right); Mikalai Nick Zastsenski, p. 11 (isolated); Composite_Carbonman, p. 13 (carbon fiber).